JORA SANKO

The Joined Bridge

Select English Poems By Bengali Poets

JORA SANKO

The Joined Bridge

Edited by: Madan G Gandhi & Kiriti Sengupta

The Poetry Society of India
Gurgaon - 122 002 (Haryana)
www.thepoetrysocietyofindia.com

Copyright: Respective poets, included in this collective effort

Cover artist: Tamojit Bhattacharya, Calcutta (India).

POETRY (ENGLISH)

ISBN: 9789383888115
Price: INR 230.00 (Rs. Two Hundred and Thirty Only)
US Dollar: $28.00

Published by:

The Poetry Society of India

H-23/16, DLF Phase-I,
Gurgaon - 122 002 (Haryana), India
Phone : 0124-4054392, 098118-42292
Email : thepoetrysoindia@gmail.com,
mgwebguru@gmail.com
Website : www.thepoetrysocietyofindia.com

JORA SANKO

The name 'Jora Sanko' reminds us of the *Jorasanko Thakur Bari*, house of the *Thakurs* (anglicized to Tagore), located in the northern part of Calcutta. This is actually the ancestral home of Rabindranath Tagore, who was born and had spent his childhood days in this house. Until now Tagore is the only Bengali poet to have received the Nobel Prize in literature. He received the honor for his English rendition of the Bengali poetry, *Gitanjali*.

Editing *Jora Sanko* has been a wonderful experience. I did some similar work in one of my books, *The Reciting Pens* (published by Inner Child Press, limited, U.S.A.) that included three contemporary Bengali poets and the interviews that I held with them. The book bore a few of their poems, which I translated into English. I remember that the noted poet W.F. Lantry (Washington, DC) wrote this in the foreword: "...we don't know enough about contemporary Bengali poets, and we should. Yes, we all love Tagore, and maybe we have read a little of Kazi Nazrul Islam, if we've been lucky, we have sampled Shanka Ghosh. But we are far more likely to know the tradition from which contemporary Bengali poetry draws its strength: the *Mahabharata*, the *Bahgavad Gita*, the *Vedas*, the *Sufis*..." (Ref: *The Reciting Pens*, page no. vi, ISBN: 9780615861869)

Prior to explaining our motto I must say that literary workers across the globe are not so aware of the Bengali poetic heritage. Here again I will quote an excerpt from *The Reciting Pens* as I had probed the poet Suddhasatya Ghosh about his take on this issue. Ghosh had been elaborate in his answer, but I would rather like to put down this: "...Hopefully you are aware that Bankim Chandra and Madhusudan Dutt had written in English during their early literary career. That was way before Rabindranath. But they were silently ignored and so were the others who wrote after them or had translated their works into English until 1947. The Rulers tried to keep themselves up above the ruled. After 1947 (post independence) it was a bit different issue altogether. Although we had our own government, we had almost a no-show in the international market. If you closely watch the development of Indian English authors you will find out that neither Salman Rushdie nor V. S. Naipaul can be considered among the Indian English authors. Vikram Seth, Amitav Ghosh or Chetan Bhagat arrived after a long period. It all began when a few Indian companies and/or International publishers considered the Indian domestic market seriously. Taru Dutt (1856-77), an Indian English poet-cum-novelist (she wrote a novel in French) with some renown was not evaluated properly at her time, yet Arundhati Roy received Booker in 1998. This is quite a long journey, and if it is the Indian scenario of English literature then what can be expected from the translations done from the native languages?" (Ref: *The Reciting Pens*, page no. 51)

Here in this anthology our aim was to compile select works (in English language) of the contemporary Bengali poets. No translations, but poetry that was primarily written in English. We had numerous submissions, but we were absolutely strict in our selection. The final result is now to be evaluated by the readers and critics. I'm confident of the contributing poets, and I am sure that their works, as contained in the following chapters will speak for themselves! Unfortunately we could not include all well-known poets, for we had to rely on the electronic communications, and that not everybody was available on the World Wide Web. Again, we had a definite time-frame, but I think that we have been considerably successful in our attempt. Let me congratulate and thank all the contributing poets for trusting my vision. I am indeed grateful to Jaydeep Sarangi, Sudeep Sen and Madan G. Gandhi for supporting me in this endeavor.

Thank you,

Kiriti Sengupta
Secretary-cum-Editor,
The Poetry Society of India, Gurgaon (Haryana, India)
25th of March, 2014.

List Of Contents

Aju Mukhopadhyay, Pondicherry, India, is an award winning bilingual poet and author. His poems and stories have been widely anthologised and translated. His essays have been published in more than 40 books. He is in the editorial boards of many important magazines. Eight books contain discussions on his poetry. His Japanese style of verses abounds in international ezines and some magazines with two books of such poems published. He has three books of short stories published in Bangla and two in English. One of his short stories has been published in a Collection of Indian Short Stories in German language. He has recently been awarded Albert Camus Centenary Writer's award. His two forthcoming books are: *Manhood, Grasshood and Birdhood* (10th book of poems) and *The Story of India's Progress* (mostly on the present position of India).

India The Mother

Mother India has snow capped Himalayan crown
She sits with her feet on sea washed by the three;
Bay of Bengal, Indian Ocean and Arabian Sea
The ancient peninsula is Bharat Mata renowned.
On her left hand is Bay of Bengal and Sundarbans
Full of history, biodiversity and maritime commerce.
Farther to the north-east the land is rich
In biodiversity, wildlife and Nature's bounty.
On her right hand is the turbulent Arabian Sea with maritime
history;
Foreign merchants and missionaries from an early age
Reached attracted by the spicy smell, carrying Christ's message.
The rest of India, secured by coasts and mountains,
Is equally rich in natural wealth, holy breath and sweetness.

Humans of different faith color and race
With quest for adventure and zest for life
Charmed by her noble face
Mingled with her pristine body of humanity.
Some outsiders ravished her time and time again
Some pseudo-civilized people tried to establish their reign;
None is here now; it is India with her people sovereign.
The perpetrators of crime were from the other age;
None presently is responsible but none can the past crime assuage.
Religions, racial bigotry and weak democratic structure
Divided the holy country; those are at work wreaking damage
further.

The real enemies are insiders holding powers
Who stealthily rob her wealth and beauty; the cheaters.
But Mother the mighty will ruin the rogues, stop the trend
To give birth to unity
In accord with her inner harmony
And wholesome spirituality.

With all admixtures India is a cauldron of culture;
Present looks back to greet the past
Past comes back to harmonize the present;
With all imports and revivals, looking to the future
India is unique in her original essence.
Let all those who left come back to make a single race.
Let all try to fulfill themselves in her racticing
With a heart vibrant and roseate.
In peace let India shine among the nations
To fulfill her mission of creating a world United.

The Events

Last of them, a couple, left an hour before noon
it started from the second midday
in a two-day literary festival;
taking leave one by one.
The third is a no-program Sunday
many left in the morning flight
alone I stay put
in the vacant guest house;
a hiatus after tremendous hullabaloo
as if nothing happened in the past two days;
a gulf of silence
island of non-existence
nothing prevails:
No talks no grudge no banter or smile
no hearty laughter or impatience senile.
All impressions and remembrances
as if in a faded film
dumped in the waste-bin of time.
Life after life
events after events
it has been happening;
everything is in a flux
everything flows into the void
yet they take place
the evanescent events.

Invisibly With Me

With a soft touch caressing
whispering blushing
sometimes with a rude shock
a foreboding experience
other times like a friendly fondle
a remembrance of the idle days
over a cup of tea;
it meets me in various ways
flowing over me, through me
coming out of the doors of the body.
It behaves differently at different times
as its nature changes seasonally;
endearingly, roughly, lovingly
telling me of its presence constantly.
Its presence at different parts of the body
is conspicuous at different stages of life.
Flowing in and out of my nostrils
the air as breath
supports me essentially
to live.

The Grasshood

just few leaves
few stems and seeds
with light body
humble under feet
mowed by machine
neglected like street urchin
but head always high
grass lives and dies and lives
feeds innumerable herbivores
who are food to carnivores;
grass like paddy undulating in moonlight
feeds millions of men and mice
grass like wheat feeds the hungry human tide
grass like bamboo covers large chunks of wood
raising its head high, characteristic of grasshood,
helping elephants rats and men to lead healthy life;
grass grows covering miles and miles
but man reduces its size
killing it with might
 telling the earth with perfect satire
that he never wishes
such trifle thing and slight
as grass to interfere
in his high-handedness,
that man can prepare
uprooters, satellites and cutters
poisonous nuclear arsenals
et al to put grass to death;
happy grass never dies
living humbly with the head high
man lives and lives
dying to himself many times
until one day to realize
that grass like earth

and wind and space
and water and fire
and breath
is superior
to man
naturally.

Asit Maitra, FRCS, Emeritus A&E consultant (Newcastle Hospitals NHS Foundation Trust), MA (Creative Writing, Newcastle University)has published two chapbooks: *Zig-Zags* (with Pat Borthwick), Pharos Press, 1998 and *Chapati-moon*, ID on Tyne Press, 2007 and four books, three of them poetry collections: *Sun Dips at Juhu Beach* (2009), *Knife on the edge* (2010), *Under the street lamp* (2011) and *Two Wings* (2012) - a collection of poems and short stories, all by Biscuit Publishing. His poems have been widely published, the latest in Let's Play! , 2014, Frances Lincoln Children's Books.

My Recipe For Creativity

Take a large piece of your empty mind
Put it on the imagination-hob
Add 3 red hot idea-seeds you have picked up
during your reading-research.
Only 1 is needed but with 3 result guaranteed
Watch them catch fire and splash
Tone down the drive-flame
Put the thinking-lid on
After 5 minutes or so add a pint of clichés-water
Simmer for an hour, stir
occasionally with your wooden writing-mood
Check it's piping hot with the revising-tongue taster
And then serve it on the page-plate,
adding last minute garnishes of word-change
for spelling mistakes etcetera.

A Pair Of Scissors

We quarrel, two blades of a scissors.
We are in touch, then far apart,
We argue slicing our love into pieces.

We have to have separation
When we are on opposite ends
Of our political and other beliefs.

When we are on the job
We cut away bits that don't fit in.
We know what we're doing.

Many times I feared we'd be gone
And a shiny new one would be in place.
The steel edge glinting in the light.

But I know and you too,
Fancy new ones may sparkle for a time
We, the old pair would outlast all.

Bird Song

I step into my back garden
And hear a bird sing –
Clear, sharp and sweet.
I don't recognize the tune.
I look up at the tall fir tree
And its undulating leaves
But can't spot the hidden artist.
The music continues, and then stops.
Soon a flurry of feathers
And it's gone.
Was it the blackbird, our favorite,
Or a newcomer – a twit or a robin
Trying to woo me out of my mood
Or simply discover a new abode?

Walking The Streets

I walk the streets
In drizzly cold rain and sweltering heat,
Clayton Street and Dinendra Street,
Newcastle upon Tyne and Kolkata city.
My feet pound the pavements -
Broken or maintained.
Shops, restaurants, cafes,
Street vendors and beggars
Compete to catch my eye.
Sometimes I have to stop –
It's the biological clock
Telling me, take a breather.
Then walking takes over.
Doctors and friends tell me
Repeatedly, take it easy.
They think I am crazy trying to buy back
Youth and redefine my place on earth.
All I know when I go walking
I hear clearly, in spite of the urban noise,
The rhythm of my heart drumming
The rhythm of the fetus
Across time, people and places;
Old and new coalescing.

Bishnupada Ray is an Associate Professor of English at the University of North Bengal, West Bengal, India. His poetry has appeared in *Indian Literature, New Quest, Makata, A Hudson View Poetry Digest, Shabdaguchha* and *Revival.* He won a Pushcart Prize nomination in 2009. His latest book of poetry *White Lotus and Other Poems* was published by Adhyayan publishers, New Delhi in 2014.

Coalition

my life is a coalition
of forces I cannot govern
they keep me under pressure
accuse me of misdeeds
threaten to desert me
and reduce me to a minority
so at my centre there are
weakness misrule corruption
dithering and bad reputation
yet govern I must
because in my survival or fall
I am the only stakeholder.

Remix

in the realm of a question mark
the breathing spaces are marked
by pauses and semi-colons
so life holds on tenuously
the video has stopped
so the monitor goes to sleep
but the audio never stops
it restarts from the beginning
so it makes the impression
that nothing is perhaps too old
or one must face the music daily
so that cruel memory becomes crueler
and we drag our exclamations
to her treasure box of spam
that overflows like menstruation
till we bracket our poor sentiments
in the state of mental menopause.

Scarecrow

I am imputed with
scaring the crow
but I am myself
a tattered cloth
upon a stick
and an empty vessel
for a head
and a painted face
as I am vandalized
by the crows of night
this midnight frost
this frozen field
of unnecessary pain
scares my lonely soul.

Menagerie

my doll's house is crumbling
but my glass menagerie
has survived the Russian winter
it is springtime now
and my glass animals
are sprucing their feathers
or softening their fur
they are glowing
with the new sun
before they can get ready
for the mind-forged monsters
to come and shatter them.

SUDEEP SEN [www.sudeepsen.net] is widely recognized as a major new generation voice in world literature and 'one of the finest younger English-language poets in the international literary scene' (*BBC Radio*). Sen's prize-winning books include: *Postmarked India: New & Selected Poems* (HarperCollins), *Distracted Geographies, Rain, Aria* (A K Ramanujan Translation Award), *Ladakh,* and *The HarperCollins Book of English Poetry* (editor). *Blue Nude: New & Selected Poems | Translations 1979-2014* (Jorge Zalamea International Poetry Prize) is forthcoming from Partridge | Penguin Random House. His poems, translated into twenty-five languages, have featured in major international anthologies. His words have appeared in the *Times Literary Supplement, Newsweek, Guardian, Observer, Independent, Telegraph, Herald, Harvard Review, Hindu, Hindustan Times, Times of India, Outlook, India Today,* and broadcast on BBC, PBS, CNN IBN, NDTV,AIR *&Doordarshan*. Sen's newer work appears in *New Writing 15* (Granta), *Language for a New Century* (Norton), *Leela* (Collins), *Indian Love Poems* (Knopf/Random House/Everyman), *Out of Bounds* (Bloodaxe), and *Initiate: Oxford New Writing* (Blackwell). He is the editorial director of AARK ARTS and the editor of *Atlas.*

Sen is the first Asian to be honored with an invitation to participate at the 2013 Nobel Laureate Week in St Lucia, where he delivered the Derek Walcott Lecture and read his own poetry. A special commemorative edition of his work, *Fractals: New & Selected Poems | Translations 1978-2013*, was released by the Nobel laureate Derek Walcott himself in the presence of H.E. Dame Pearlette Louisy, Governor General (President) of St Lucia. The same year, the Government of India Ministry of Culture's awarded him the senior fellowship for "outstanding persons in the field of culture."

GAAYIKA'R CHITHI:
Nine Movements from a Singer's Score sheet

> *Ami aakashe patiya kaan,*
>   *Sunechi, sunechi tomari gaan,*
> *Ami tomare shoonpeeechi praan,*
>   *O go bideshini! ...*
> — RABINDRANATH TAGORE,
>   'Ami Chini Go Chini Tomare'

> *Though we're apart,*
> *You're part of me still.*
> — FATS DOMINO, 'Blueberry Hill'

Bideshini, Banalata

I dream of pink and cream *dhakai* colours,
  of crisp-starched *sari* and honey-inflected throat —
a voice modulating *tulsi,* cloves and warm water
  to keep Rabindra Sangeet scales pitch-perfect.

I dream of Dhaka and longing, longing for
  that beautiful connect with my father's soil
and my child's early childhood — of Banani,
  Sonargaon, Faridpur; of Boi Mela, Chobi Mela;

of the long afternoons months-on-end at
  Samshur Rahman's book-filled Shyamoliroom—
his wild silver hair and mischievous smile
  guiding my hands as I translated his poetry

from Bangla to English — syllable by syllable,
  word by word, phrases strung together to make
music in a new tongue. But tonight, I mostly
  dream of music — how its hidden heart-strings

bind and grace a friendship. "We are blessed —
   Allah-ki-duaey hain"—I tell my friend —
wet-lips, saliva, empty railway platforms,
   endless hot cups of tea, stories, dreams —

recipes for poetry and song. We are lucky
   to be graced with muse's magic, lucky to fuel
a spontaneous combustion, if only partially.
   I dream of Bideshini with fresh white *champa*

petals pinned askance on her night-black hair,
   her pupils reflecting the well-worn Gitabitan —
its Bangla fonts and typefaces — lyrics imprinted
   like invisible tattoos on her salt wheat skin.

Though we're apart, you're part of me still —
   I remember you Banalata, my Bideshini.
This winter night in Delhi is crisp as a song
   and sheer — as glass is— when dreaming.

Jessore

I have lived in a golden cage — caged and tamed.
                    I am mostly lost.

When I dive headlong
into the bracing winter winds —
              chill greets my face —
it is electric.

In my village,
I remember diving into the old cold pond
           blanketed by a layer of thick moss —
my naked skin, comforted by green velvet.

Delhi

After a long concert, and after dinner,
I find myself unexpectedly with you
                              in my room.

In this new space
                  finding oneself is wonderful,
you say.

I was here and not here at the same time.

Later, I felt as if I had entered a story
                  of an old familiar novel,
        a character I knew
                        but had not met in flesh
        until now —
        you, me, and my winter's dream.

Dhaka

Today's wintry morning sun
                    is like frosted glass.

I am happy
            cocooned in my embryo.

Nothing has happened —
no, everything has happened —
                        no —

yet I am getting carried away
                    by the toasted air
of this new season.

                    My heartstrings conduct
the tenor and pitch
        of a song
            I no longer have control of.

Light as air,
        the inflected phrases
waft in my imagined new home
                    with you —

alone, together, and all alone—
smiling, kissing,
                    kissing, and kissing —
            you are my song.

Nowadays

all seems bright
  and energetic to me —

as if the winter fog
  has cleared it way

for sharp sunlit bracing
  days and nights.

Everything is lucid
  and crystalline —

colours over-saturated,
  weather perfect,

my hidden smile
  now unhidden.

I laugh openly, loudly,
  and so much more.

I sing open-throated
  in sheer abandon.

My dreams are
  kaleidoscopic, vivid,

and my words now
  always gentle.

I have escaped from
  my old gold cage

just for a while,
  but this while feels

like a lifetime —
  and it is a gift

I am grateful for.
  So I sing — and sing.

Winter Evening

Through the thicket
  and thickset clumps

of tropical groves —
  of mango, banana,

coconut and *kathaal* —
  the winter evening

sun pierces
  its molten gold rays.

Streaks of sunlight
  try to illuminate

a*mis-en-scene*
  that goes unnoticed

to an everyday eye.
  This light's

tempered heat —
  not too hot,

not too cold —
  caresses my skin,

its minute subtle
  calibrations

played out with care.
  The amber light

bathes my body and
  casts variable shadows

on my white couch —
  the patterns

changing
  every millisecond

as the sun starts to dip.
  Right now,

the white cushions
  are dappled

and patterned by
  furtively left

gold-red lipstick
  marks

after the lovers
  have beaten

a hasty retreat.
  Even though

soon it will be dark
  and these shadows

on the love-seat
  would disappear,

the lovers
  will carry with them

only what they
  wish to carry

in their mind's heart —
  the designs

created by the heat
  and light —

always lit at the
  perfect temperature,

and always
  beautifully poised,

just the way
  the two people

wish it to be —
  soft-frozen in time.

Remembrance

Red sheds her skin
  to reveal pink tonight —

the dawn-pink reflected
  on the building

wall's canvas
  opposite my room.

Colours blush
  mimicking my heart —

their new song
  altering lyrics to melt

madness to sanity,
  sense to sensibility.

Burkha's hidden stories
  are now unveiled —

imprinted beautifully
  on your sari's raw red.

Question

Your body scent
  and strands of long

night-kissed hair
  left on my pillow —

broken blouse-buttons
  on my bed-sheet —

a disengaged
  lone eyelash

curved, left behind
  as a question mark —

What happened? —
  Beauty.

Reflecting quicksand,
  mirrors of time —

my *answers* live
  in your punctuations.

Shiuli

*Ek mutho shishir bheja
  shiuli pathalam ...*— SR

S*hiuli* flowers, slow-warmed
  in your clenched fists,

drenched in morning dew
  greets me with the scent

of your soft palm, fingers,
  and heartstrings. I weave

these tiny flowers, petal by petal,
  threading their stamen

filament by filament,
  into a delicate garland —

inking a love song's score
  in handwritten script.

Unknown to me,
  you'll wear these florets

in your silk-raven hair, and
  around your slender wrists;

singing my new song —
  Tagore as your witness —

tonight, and every night.

Debasish Lahiri teaches English literature at Lal Baba College, under the University of Calcutta. He has also taught widely at the Post-Graduate and M.Phil level at several universities. His writings on Postcolonial theory, American Poetry, and European Modernism have been published in international journals and books. His poems have also been widely published in journals like The Journal of the Poetry Society of India, Muse-India, Inkapture from Durham, U.K, The Poetry Salzburg Review &c. His first book of poems *First Will And Teastament* was published from Writers Workshop in 2012. He is working on his second book of 'travel' poems. He is also a reviewer and regular contributor to the Life & Letters column of The Statesman, Kolkata.

Night-Watch

Trust me
It was darkness visible:
The nipped bud of a cigarette,
Amber ember,
That pouted still at the dark.
I walk slowly at night,
Uncertain,
Threatened by that long barrel of noise
That is called civilization.
But, like this street-lamp,
Fast asleep on its watch,
The barrel droops,
The trigger-finger slackens
And no longer is the city
The bully with its grip firmly
Shackling both light and darkness.
I wade through the darkness of streets
And raise no ripple of light;
My silhouette darkened by the moon,
Like beauty's aspect by a voyeur.
The drum-roll of canine desires
Ushers my entrance onto the high street.
I feel canonized by St. Rembrandt.
I feel canonized in the glorious umbrage,
His handiwork.
I imagine the heft of the officer-of-the-watch
In the howls that are raised
By the dark. My gait changes,
From a prowl to a prance.
Tall, silent houses allow me
To view their daily curetted walls:
The banyan roots and their mandrake variations,
The heraldry of unselfconscious days,
The boast of an art that knows

Its futurelessness.
I am allowed to walk
Through these museums of the street,
Museums where the nights of days are preserved;
Where led by the kindly light
I often fearfully look up to shadows of magnitude,
Sky-wide and colorless.
And all this while
The expectoration of the seasons
Is kind to me
In a damp sort of way.
I walk carefully
Past the house of Croesus,
Careful not to rouse the rich man
To the barking of his own dogs,
Who bark at the night,
That beggar at his gates.
But I am Cophetua too tonight.
Beggar, with a pot of gold
And the prospect of a beggar,
Gently grating against the street's wishes
For that beggar-girl,
Love.
Impossible to recognize,
Darker than both the night and me,
(The cowl of our shadows thrown in too),
Powerful like the plea of million-atom'd dust
That my relentless feet drag along,
Love
Will surely crown me with sprigs of darkness
Honed to a keenness by the memory of thorns.
But the streets will not allow
This skull that sprouted nettles to take the air
And the street lamps shall, I think,
Herod-like be wise to it.
One more turn

And I seem to have come into a cave of light
With flocks of people
Like moths threatening the light,
Dying around it.
My journeys are at an end.
I have carried the night like a dark cleft in my temple
With my eyes shut to the light.
I see better by darkness as the street does,
Or the museum,
When all the lights go out.

Galleries In The Night

Abandoned by all kindly lights
To gnash their teeth
In penumbras of their own making,
What half-bitten talk
Peoples the dark galleries
Between masterpiece and masterpiece,
Restrained from lawless combat
By gilt-edged police
Or the girth of mortar?
The greatest allegories of art
Are secret journals kept
By that gossip Night
Whom no historian of art consults
As they measure time by daylight;
Though the essence of all art
Is what the twilight leaves behind in the hall,
Is the closing of the gate,
And drawing up of the bridge,
Is the third watch and the owl
And all things that dream of the soul
When the fires have burnt down,
But not the night.

Dodging December By The Apocalyptic Route

So what is it that waits for you
In the sun? –
The changing form
Of your unchanging shadow:
A bronze evening face
That catches the sun
And is unmoved,
The granite Indian
Behind the black rock
In the great American dime novel.

What is it that waits for you
In the shade?
A soul,
That dreams like a body
Of ink:
Apollinaire's octopus,
Blood thirsty, ink-thrifty,
Blood turned to ink;
Treble-hearted monster,
Great feeder of suffering.

Once I saw four men killed[**]
By the same truth,
Death.
They were all dancers.
Death danced briefly
In three out-of-breath bodies
That fell out of tune
With desire;
The fourth was a death
By recollection.
That was Art.

And then I saw four men kill
A truth,
Life.
Life was swilled in sweat
And leant slightly like the four Pisan towers
Around it,
Before the snap
Of broken sap
Of a woman's neck and waist,
The gum oozing
Down the broken stalk.
A snap like a thunderclap
In a wordless forest
Where even the wind
Ran mad with nightmare in its hair.

Four men on a beautiful night
Cooed like a heavenly bull
That had bored Europa's thighs
With embers of divine desire.
Death by God,
Or death by Death,
A woman's choice,
Life's choice,
Apocalypse through history.
This is art too.

The merry men have danced again.
A deathless dance,
A satyr's trance
On a beautiful night
When sorrow gurgled like a nameless river
Sweeter than Alpheus.

Let us go then,
You and I,

People of the soul,
Survivors from a planet
Called Life
Where deep mines in our buried bodies
Are ringing with soft, hot, pink, inexpressible
Surges of a pain
That is music to the spheres.

Put a finger on your lips.
Let us remind ourselves
That it is the soul's nature
To be inward,
Muttering, holding its tongue,
While the body crackles with fat and words.
Today,
In this long funeral of the body
The soul is active,
Quirking eloquent protest,
Drowning the bored wait of the body
With peals of silence,
As loud as drum-rolls in cities,
Or barbarian battle-cries
In empty Roman porches.

Let us go then to this funeral of the body,
A woman, bored,
Waiting out the soulful verbiage
Of days
Till her heart gave way
And the battered body
No longer buffeted
The silent hosannas of the soul.

So,
What is it that waits for me
In the sun,

Tomorrow?
A woman,
My body, Me.
And what is it that waits for me
In the shade?
My soul, a man,
With whom I shall grow poor and full
Of words
That sound like that hush in God's noisy wake.

January, 2013 [** Pablo Picasso's "Three Dancers"]

Ever-a-Day

Wet rock, Waiting dryly in prose, Granular grammar, For the
warm rain, Promised, But lost in waiting To words That it dropped
On my million year old palm.
The song of a furtive sun
Rises above the white clouds,
Hard and ringingly silent
Under brown trees,
And falls beneath the wood-hen's chuckle:
The fox has caught a kinetic death,
Carried along through a penumbra
That promised, briefly, a world beyond time.
On the lizard-ledge of the bristly afternoon
The last Cain smiles for my critic-gaze:
One thing alone does not exist–
Oblivion.

Hyderabad, December 2013

Debjani Chatterjee was born in Delhi, grew up in several Asian countries and studied Comparative Literature, Religious Studies, Education and Psychotherapy at five universities in Egypt and Britain. She has been called 'Britain's best-known Asian poet' (Elisabetta Marino) and 'a national treasure' (Barry Tebb). Her 60+ books for children and adults include *I Was That Woman, Words Spit and Splinter* and *Namaskar: New and Selected Poems*. Her prize-winning books include: *Barbed Lines, The Redbeck Anthology of British South Asian Poetry* and *Rainbow World*. A former Chair of the National Association of Writers in Education and the Arts Council of England's Translations Panel, she is a Royal Literary Fellow at Leeds Trinity University and Associate Editor of *Pratibha India*. She is a patron of Survivors' Poetry, Co-Chair of the mental health charity Hyphen-21 and founder of The Healing Word and Bengali Women's Support Group. Her writing residencies have included ones at Sheffield Children's Hospital, Ilkley Litfest and York St John University. Her many awards include Sheffield Hallam University's honorary doctorate for 'outstanding contribution to Literature, the Arts and Community Service' and an MBE in the Queen's Honours list 2008. She was an Olympic Torchbearer in 2012.

Web: www.debjanichatterjee.moonfruit.com

A Tribute to Mahmoud Darwish
(after visiting his tomb and museum, 26th October 2013)

It was a brave thing you did, Mahmoud,
though a simple word. You said:
'I am an Arab'.
Millions kissed you on both cheeks.

It was a hard way to live, Mahmoud,
though a noble hope. You said:
'We are both human'.
Billions hold you in their hearts.

Kanagawa Tanka
*(inspired by Katsushika Hokusai's 'The Great Wave off
Kanagawa')*

Tsunami rises
off Kanagawa; hail stones
crash on beach and boat.
Snow-flecked waves claw fishing rafts.
Fujiyama meditates.

Perfect Fusion

You too juggle two lives:
your humdrum daily yawn
and that other of vivid dreams
when you somersault and fly.

So my two selves are a part of me,
my humanity and my fishy tail
are perfectly fused – look!
you cannot find the seamless
join at my supple waist.
Which of your selves do you see
reflected in my gleaming scales?
Which of your lives do you dream?
Questions, for me, as meaningless
as an oceanic murmuring.
You prattle of half this and half that,
you admire the grip of starfish on my breasts,
the coral and seashell necklace
that I made to nestle between them,
and crinkle your nose at my wet fish smell;
but when I look into the twin mirror
of your eyes, I see a balanced whole –
I am a mermaid.

Halfie
(For Shipra)

Terms like 'half-breed', 'cross-breed', 'half-caste'
mulatto, mongrel, mixed
leave us in a vacuum of no man's land -
they are neither here nor there.
But I'm half with that anthropologist,
Palestinian-American, Abu-Lughod,
who described herself as a 'halfie.'
Halfie - a good word to reflect on.
When we have two lands we are halfies
whose two halves are both more
and less than the sum of their parts;
marriages outside our communities
make us cosmopolitan, international, halfies;
teenagers are halfies who have a foot each
in caterpillar childhood and winged adult age;
grey hair with its in-between dark and white pronounces us halfies
in a visible way.
As global survivors, we are all halfies
navigating paths between birth and death.
Halfies endure the worst of both worlds
- and enjoy the best.

Note:
Lila Abu-Lughod, a professor of Anthropology and Women's
Studies, coined the term 'halfie.'

Gopal Lahiri was born and grew up in Kolkata. A post graduate in Geology, he works as a geoscientist and currently lives in Mumbai, India.He is a bilingual poet, writer, editor and translator and widely published in Bengali and English language. His English poetry books include *Silent Steps* and *Living Inside* and four POD books published by Lulu, USA. His translation works in Bengali *Not Just Milk and Honey*, (published by *NBT, India*), a collection of short stories of Israel is widely acclaimed. Anthology appearances (among others) includes *National Treasures, Indus Valley, A posy of poesy, Concerto, Poet's paradise, The Silence within, Indo-Australian Anthology, The Dance of the Peacock, Illuminations, Inklink, Poets International*. His works have featured in many journals: *Indian Literature, Taj Mahal Review, CLRI, Haiku Journal* and electronic publications *Arts and Letters, Underground Window, Muse India, Poetry Stop, Debug*. He has jointly edited the anthology *Scaling Heights*. He was awarded the acclamation of 'Highly Commended' in the Poet of the Year Category of the Destiny Poets' International Community of Poets *ICOP Awards 2012 and 2013, Wakefield, U.K.* He can be reached at glahiri@gmail.com *and* gopallahiri.blogspot.com

Canvas

In my eyes, it is so obvious
along the bright lines,
sync with colors.

set of her shoulder
tilt of the forehead
look in her round eyes.

life in a plastic bubble
under the brutal sun
in the waves of whirling dust.

it's always worth asking
for her close attention
what is the gist of existence?

the long nose and the abrupt curve
on the undulating forehead,
haunted, immutable.

speed, force and movement
there they all are,
glowing on canvas.

Speak In Your Voice

Let me speak in your voice
soft, tenderly, caring,
erasing my brashness.

gone are the stressful sound blasts
it's only the fibers,
that mellows the rough edges.

humming to the tune of green moss
they may well be at the tip of the river,
or sit at the top of the wet wood
feel like balances it out.

but in your voice
they may be sonorous
solid tone with no sharp tremolo
but that doesn't speak my language.

my empty voice, wound and pain
tears with bloodstain
it's really for struggle every time
walk on the marble or granite.

I tried hard but reality never fits in
I am not, I am not you,
there is really no soul
in your voice.

Showdown

Each page of the book revising
learning the wilderness inside,
toothy smile and dusty look
denting the shadows

the way everything conjures
feathers and blood, fighting birds
gliding close to the surface
we are promised a showdown.

the way the evening sky
bundles its low clouds
in shimmering desert
when you sow the seeds of doubt.

they all are looming over
to catch the tiny branches
hidden behind the two hands
intimate, personal, running for pleasure.
.
respond to it, even to crave it
for the rare earth model
I really don't know what to do until
you are doing it.

Escape

Somewhere in the tunnel
the lights disappear into the beaten track,
in moments like these of a journey
that begins to look for outstretched hands
survive in the lowermost reaches.

the odd resonance of the unknown voice
on the jagged edges of the stone wall,
reaches out only in the aching soul
eyes not seen, feel only the laterite soil
scatter in heaps, block the rugged path.

the search for tiny holes for passage of light
too long; surely will not be tolerated
it's time to fall asleep and draw the radius
of the distance to allow the escape from
the long knives of teeming darkness.

Jaydeep Sarangi is a scholar, poet, translator and critic. His pen chronicles a new history of the downtrodden, his personal pangs and sorrows, his day to day life in a busy metro city as well as his happy celestial days of creativity. For him, life of a poet enjoys a full promise between the outer world and the creative self. Widely anthologized and reviewed as a bilingual poet, he authors three poetry collections in English and one in Bengali. His latest book of poems in English, *Silent Days* was released at the Westerly Centre, UWA, Perth in the Summer 2013. His fourth book of English poems (***A Door-Somewhere?)*** will be released during his upcoming academic trip to Poland in April-May 2014. About his poems Keki Daruwalla, one of the leading Indian writers in English and the recipient of the Sahitya Akademi Award says "Jaydeep Sarangi gives a fresh paint to everyday living. 'Small rivers' near tribal villages are his haunts. His language can be unorthodox, where a rock can turn into a 'reckless flow,' but his poems are a rewarding read, with the scent of herbs coming through the pages." Dr. Paula Hayes (USA) in her Introduction to the book, *From Dulong to Beas* (New Delhi,2012) says, "a few of Jaydeep's poems reach toward asking metaphysical questions." "As we all know, India has a rich literary tradition. Jaydeep Sarangi is a splendid member of this endless family. Truly, a poet of note," exclaims Dora Sales of the University JaumeI, Castellón, Spain. Dr. Jaydeep Sarangi is the Associate Professor in English, Deptt. of English at Jogesh Chandra Chaudhuri College (Calcutta University), 30,Prince Anwar Shah Road, Tollygunj; Kolkata-700033, India.

Baby Growing In A Poet

Death has different meanings for us at different stages of life
So is poetry.
Its images are collage
Of thoughtful ideas wedded into a door,
Symbols are its bricks and stones
Of a home of thoughts,
Where nerves make a man grow
Like a poem
Beginning, middle and an end.
'I revise quite a lot,' says a veteran poet.
The fragile erotic moments of love, lust and of touch
Come and go,
dream of a rivulet where tribal women are splashing away in the rain water
poetry captures them in sweet cadence.

It's a movement in men,
A bubble of desire
That leaps water
As black cloud does in monsoon.
Poetry is close to heart
It moves hearts,
Extends things further
Where colorful mosaics
Drag sensations from bricks and metals.

Lovers have a day,
In rhymed thoughts.
An art form may predate <u>literacy</u>
Beside a rivulet
Far away from the city's rust.
Life rides on words!

When She Is Gone With The Wind
(In memory of a pet)

On its flashy wardroom
a flashy woman
pushes her pet

Life's lean rod in rainy days,
wet.

Golden light flashes
from the other direction
as her kisses spur
Its journey to some evolved form
in another time.

Move on little friend
just pause and feel
you're cradled still

Faith makes her strong
there begins the wait
to greet him back
in form renewed

With lessons learned
her bosom prepares
to serve again

Somewhere
We also count days

as **she** says,
road to evolution.

New Year Gift!

By the glass doors somewhere
you kneel, wait for another new year.
Your colored body shapes a figure against the sky.
A yellow leaf falls from the mango tree.
I see a flesh of rust-red, crawling somewhere.
I notice the steady rise and fall
of your bare brave chest.
I hold myself back, only to reason—
each passing moment where an untouchable dies
In front of an elite,
On the banks of the Ganges
Pale skinned, the smell of death
Eyes vacant and dull.

I guess I repeat
Myself: pray for my proud birth.
Your blood unfurls that history
I have written over generations.
I save my ancestors as you save your missing links.

When the crows fly over, your brothers listen.

Beyond The Walls

Oh! Stop me near its blind end
where the dream ends.
It's to feel as if it moves on to the eggs of eternity.
I bleed as I was not born as a stone,
a Perfect stone.

Though it's not for my whole life
of a bard,
yet go on with obvious manifestations.
After a sweet spell, it becomes close to my metal wire,
When some of my fellowmen eat boiled rice
and invent walls
in-between soft zones
where love kisses souls,
I step in to a lighted halo.
Walls are doors
into things.

Ranadeb Dasgupta belongs to Barasat, Calcutta. He is a high school physics teacher and enjoys his brilliant fan-following from being a poet. One of his translated poems has been published in *Twist of Fate*, produced by Stephen L Wilson, U.S.A. Ranadeb enjoys several Bengali publications in e-zines and in little magazines. His first Bengali poetry book, *Kobitabela Shono (Listen O Poetic Spell)* was published some eight years back. His second poetry book, *Doyatera Lupto Hoye Gechhe (The Ink-pots Turned Redundant)* has been a major hit among the Bengali poetry lovers, and it is now slated for its second edition. Ranadeb's poetry was published in *Heaven Above: Poetry Below*, a poetry anthology by Brian Wrixon, Canada. He has been featured in Kiriti Sengupta's nonfiction *The Reciting Pens*, published by the Inner Child Press, limited (U.S.A.).

Full-Stop

funny, you know
how can I restrict the breath
and a moving cloud
throughout the blood
that swims.

nothing is full
even nothingness not
colors are cheating
my eyes, you know.

if I kiss a stop
something begins that moment,
it's a bo-peep we do play,
for the search of a full-stop dear.

Things

soft in the morning
lost or gained by the daylong soul
I connect the self with the core
core that make out things
looks are somewhere stranger
as you look behind the sight
it seems writing the invisible
and things remain
I fly away.

Despot

are you a despot?
you speak so calm yet rude,
you smile but I hear groan
defined as you are
within a luminous spell,
I feel a mace invisible
in your palms so delicate,
an offering poison yet.

know not who you are
need not what you tell–
I accept destined way
love is a despot....well.

Digital

and finally
I was uploaded to your orbit
with a huge blue afternoon.
like a virtual bird
your wings had no sky,
not a nest even.
I touched the silent buttons,
I clicked to have a tale.
it uttered nothing
and nothingness ruled.

digitized as my letters are
it only costs your coin
not your smile indeed.

Rudra Kinshuk (b. 1971), a poet, trans-creator and critic has to his credit a number of publications in English, including *Footprints on the Sands (1996), Portrait of a Dog as Buddha (1998), Marginal Tales of the Galloping Horses (2002), Meditations on Matricide (2012)* and *Fragrant Anchors (2013)*. His poems have been translated into French and German. A collection of his poems translated into French is in print with the title *Ancres Odorantes (2013)*. He was awarded a fellowship in literature by M.H.R.D, New Delhi for research in *Santal* oral literature.

Pachyderms

Rhinos are pachyderms.
They cannot respond to rains
 easily.

In moonlight rhinos
often come out with bowls
in hands for collecting contributions.

Even in dreams, I get wonder stuck.

This age is a rhino age, thick-skinned and low-headed.
Only a great fire can bring an end to it.

Notes On Buffalos

Buffalos graze on our pastures.
They don't know
that indigo houses have memories,
so, they easily
can get themselves melted
in the soft light of morning.

While going to the market every day
I look at the grazing horses
beside the indigo house
beside the yellow pages.

In A Bakery

A burning hearth.
Elastic dough of flour
roasted
in the breath of fire.
A fragrant sword or a siren.

Jingle Bells

75

Silence needs noise, noise of many
failures misunderstood.

A bird of dream
falls on the collective leaves, withering and yellow.

The cat, always running after shadows
knows that fertile earth is meant for seeds.

Jingle-bells musicise solitude.
I know that woods of night
have distinct ears for stories of mine.

I'll have wait for the river Torsha
and the blue trees around.

Silence needs my surrender
to her embrace of effacing acceptance...

Sanjukta Dasgupta is Professor and Former Head, Dept of English and Former Dean, Faculty of Arts, Calcutta University. Recipient of the Fulbright postdoctoral fellowship and several other awards and grants, she has been invited to participate in conferences and teach/lecture at universities in the USA, UK, Europe, Canada and Australia. She was also the Chairperson of the Commonwealth Writers Prize jury panel (2003-2005). She is a poet, short story writer, critic and translator and her published books are *The Novels of Huxley and Hemingway: A Study in Two Planes of Reality*, *Responses : Selected Essays, Snapshots* (poetry), *Dilemma* (poetry), *First Language* (poetry), *More Light* (poetry)*Her Stories* (translations), *Manimahesh* (translation), *The Indian Family in Transition*(co-edited SAGE). *Media, Gender and Popular Culture in India: Tracking Change and Continuity* (Co-author, SAGE, 2012), *Tagore: At Home in the World* (Co-editor SAGE 2013), *Radical Rabindranath: Nation, Family and Gender in Tagore's Fiction and Films. (Co-author, Orient Blackswan 2013), SWADES- Tagore's Patriotic Songs (translation, Visva Bharati Publication Division, 2013), Abuse and Other Short Stories (Dasgupta Book Company, 2013)*

Shooting

Shot with a camera
Shot with a gun

Shooting for fun
Shooting to kill

Pleasurable images of violence
Desirable killing fields

Man made guns and bullets
Cameras that look like guns

Fun in a gruesome pun
Pain in the bleeding sun

Last good bye of the setting sun
Which shrinks in shame

Shudders at what devastation
It may have to illuminate next day

Ashamed, the inconsolable sun
Is scared to rise again

Darkness everywhere
As every candle is blown out

Truth lies trapped in a dungeon
Lies have nuclear fangs

The hooded serpent
Sways entranced by the charmer

The flute's monotone

Moans with

Lusty dreams of proud profit
Every twisted turn is more terrifying

Dreams of poisonous pride and pomp
Nightmares of loss and humane desires

The ground beneath the feet
Cracks open and the festering cancer glows

Acid rain singes and sears
The heart of the enduring earth.

Then a hymn rises like gossamer clouds
From incense sticks

Mercy, Karuna, Mercy, Karuna
The chorus of voices chants like tinkling temple bells

A shooting star streaks the midnight blue sky
And falls earthwards, a healing pristine touch

Pride And Politics

Here's a rainbow
At one end sits
Khap pride
At the other smiles
Gay Pride
Both used
By proud politics
Coveting instant results

Connecting the poles
Wireless wizardry
Connecting polarized minds
Is not a mortal feat
No computing cloud
Can link those who de-link Others
For profitable politics

The mortal coils
Just writhe and knot
Till knots are locked
For politics loves pride
Politics loves prejudice
Politics stands as a beacon
Seducing pride and prejudice

Pride and prejudice
Creep like ivy over
Politics' pillared stretch
User-friendly pride
Time tested user-friendly prejudice
Are trusted compatriots
Of politics of profit
What is lost?

Nothing some say
Everything says others
What is lost?
What is lost?
Someone writes on the blue ceiling overhead-
What is lost alas is
Freedom to speak
Freedom to live
Freedom to desire

Someone sighs and mourns
At the cold blooded execution
Of human rights.

Chitrangada

Princess of Manipur
Swift arrows fly from her bow
Her lithe body like a flying javelin
Zooms through the foliage

Warrior prince Arjun is her target
The arrows become flowers in her scented hair
Drugged by love and desire
Warrior princess Chitrangada
Becomes lovelorn Radha

But Arjun is insatiable
The desirable luscious fruit
Is just dessert, hunger now rises
For a glimpse of the warrior princess

That wish too is fulfilled
Chitrangada the seductress
Now becomes Arjun's partner
For better or for worse

The warrior princess's caveat
To the warrior prince melts the lines of control
Let us be equal partners in peace and war
Let us entwine arms, stand side by side

"I have many flaws and blemishes
I am a traveler in the great world-path,
My garments are dirty
And my feet are bleeding with thorns"
Softly murmured
The Bard of Santiniketan's Chitra

Powerful though in pain

The visionary poet's Chitra
The Princess of Manipur
Also the princess of the people
Scripted a mantra for every woman,
Princess or pauper-
"I am Chitra. No goddess to be worshipped, nor yet
The object of common pity to be brushed aside
Like a moth, with indifference. "

Reference:

Tagore Rabindranath "Chitra" a play in *The English Writings of Rabindranath Tagore* volume 2 New Delhi: Sahitya Akademi, 2001. The Bengali play is titled, *Chitrangada*.

Chandalika

Untouchable!
Away, away
Out of sight
Outcast Chandalika

Dalit, dalit, dalit
Trampled, tortured, terrified
Cursed Chandalika
Bewildered and helpless

Then out of the horizon
Stepped steadily towards her
The serene and sensitive monk
Ananda met Chandalika

So long invisible, untouchable
Accursed Chandalika
Doomed and damned from
The day she was born

For the first time
In her wretched miserable life
Chandalika saw a smile
A smile that was not a sneer

The monk's gentle smile
Soothed her insulted soul
Healed her humiliated pores
The caring voice asked her
For some water to slake the thirst

Water touched by a Sudra!
Unholy water contaminated
By the dalit girl's innocent touch

The voices of power and privilege

Shouted and screamed
With horror and hatred
But the monk smiled and coaxed her again
For water to slake his thirst

His imploration enabled Chandalika
To raise her head high
The smile of the merciful monk
Was like the radiance
Of a thousand suns
Brilliant and pristine

Chandalika
Dalit maiden branded and ostracized
Stigmatized by mere accident of birth
And the harsh cruelty of mankind

Bathed in the pure light
A healing balm
At last, after many centuries
Traumatized Chandalika
Could smile as times were changing at last.

March 16, 2014

Sharmila Ray went to Presidency College and Calcutta University where she majored in History and subsequently joined City College, Kolkata where she is an Associate Professor and Head of the Department of History. She has authored five books of poetry-*Earth Me And You* (Granthalaya, Kolkata 1996), *A Day With Rini* (Poetry And Art 1998), *Down Salt Water* (Poets Foundation, Kolkata1999), *Living Other Lives* (Minerva Press, New Delhi, Mumbai, London 2004), *It's Fantasy, It's Reality* (Punaschya, Kolkata 2010), *With Salt And Brine* (Yeti Publishers, Calicut 2013). She has experimented her poems with sarod (Indian string instrument) and the result is a CD- *Journey Through Poetry And Music.* Her poems, short stories and non fictional essays have appeared in various national and international magazines and journals. For a time she looked after the column *Moving Hand Writes* (Cal Times, Times Of India). She also edited *Poetry And Art*, a journal of art and poetry (1992-1998). She conducted poetry workshops and translation workshops sponsored by the British Council Kolkata, Sahitya Akademi (National Akademi of Letters) and Poetry Society India and participated in various seminars organized by Universities and private institutions. She also curated an exhibition combining paintings and poems sponsored by Alliance Francaise, Calcutta and Indian Alluminium. She was also a member of the English Board of Sahitya Akademi. She also edited *The Journal* (2012-13), a poetry journal of the Poetry Society of India. Currently she is the editor of *Poetry And Prose.* Besides this her area of interest is Cultural Studies. She had been invited to International Struga Poetry Evenings, in Macedonia International poets meet in Kerala to share stage with Ben Okri. She has been reading her poems in various parts of the country. Her poems have been translated into Hindi, Bengali, Urdu, Slovenne, Hebrew, Spanish. Currently engaged in research on a book-length study on "Culture Heritage and Preservation: Interpreting the cult of Durga" and also working on a new collection of poems.

Loosing Color

There is no dream
there is no oblivion.
I move slowly in a line of flight
blanched by dust and sand.
The air is rife with the words
'smoke'em out, smoke'em out.'
I have no one to talk to
everything is divided,
even my poetry book.
Each page, each friend is a dried butterfly
pasted beautifully, loosing color.
I stagger rootlessly from one page to another.
I see a fire escape looming out of my anguish.
But where does it lead to?
Will it penetrate the mindless deceptions and
reveal unmirrored space?
Will it delete all those outsized disjunted words?
Will my grey heavy look get a twinkle?

There's no going back to childhood
and from childhood to the safety
of the womb.
I have no wish to be the silent hero of my life.
I write for you as I write for myself
even though you'll never read these words.

But watch out.
Someday the ants will attack.
There will be cloudburst and landless limbo
and when you open the door
a mummified hand of a child
will be there to greet you.

Words

Alphabets jumble words mingle
as I start writing a poem.
Long lines of words.
As I go on talking to you
they are words compressed.
As you listen to me
they are words reticent.
My thoughts are silent words.
Your smile
a wide beautiful word.
And words have colors too-
coral, topaz, cerulean.
Words breathe, words speak.
Sometimes, dust settles on words
and they become heavy, engraving on hearts.
But when words loose sound
and become deep seas within us,
then the secrets of the universe
are told in whispers.

Ruins

Naked and immense
The ruins stare at me.
Here the evenings are still born children
And the rain if falls at all is
light as a grasshopper.
I have my notions about other ruins,
but this one makes me search myself.
Each cry I utter is lost in the limitless space
then it gathers speed and hits the
frozen walls breaking into an echo.

Perhaps, the story I'm looking for
is buried beneath the mosaics and
in the whispering of the lizards.
Perhaps, it is there when the
first star shines and the
gods of night draw their curtain
over moon-drenched pillars.

Chew

The long sleek pack of Alpenlibe toffee chocolates; I hold it
between my fingers.
The thumb injecting a lot of my warmth making it more sweet and
delightful.
I give it to him before I leave station .I leave a little bit of me in all
of those brown
rounds wrapped in cellophane.

Take one of these everyday and remember me, for I'll be in their
color and flavor
In their presence and absence when you have rolled the brown
delight inside your mouth, sucking it's sweet blood and chewing
with your molar, I'll be there. And when you are in a distant mood,
your mouth caressed by a rich golden flavor, bringing out the
deeper shades of longing, I'll be there.
I'll be there when you're sitting on a road side bench with brown
exhausted leaves all around you, your absent minded feet probably
playing a tattoo with a polythene carry
bag or a crust of bread that the sparrows have left. Since it's humid
the sweat that would trickle down your spine would carry my
presence. Probably not the best of time, but still I'll be there in the
warm haze.
You'll sit unarrived, unclaimed, the passing traffic a faraway
rumble in your ears.

You can have your pick-
Shipwreck on an unknown island or the Carribean coast. Or
you can sit on that road side bench, walk with me leaving behind a
taste of bitter chocolate.

Sonnet Mondal is an Indian poet and the founder of *The Enchanting Verses Literary Review*. He has authored eight collections of poetry; his most recent book being Prismatic Celluloid (Authorspress India). His works have been featured in several publications including *The Sheepshead Review (University of Wisconsin, Green Bay)*, *The Stremez*, *India Today*, *Nth Position*, *Fox Chase Review*, *The Penguin Review* (Youngstown State University), *Two Thirds North* (Stockholm University), *California State Poetry Quarterly* (California State Poetry Society), *Dark Matter Journal*(University of Houston-Downtown) and *Friction Magazine* (New Castle University) to name a few.

Details of his works can be found at *www.sonnetmondal.com*

The Smile Loan

A gold washed reflection leaves me golden
and from her smile, I was looking good.
An impatient pair of feet continues jogging
with a long lasting smile loaned from hers.
New fruits on the mango tree of our garden
as I reached;
a strong smell of tea, cookies and faded wind
quite familiar as the daily bath
interrogates my cheeks filled with smile
for they are accustomed with a tired 'me'
gasping for a mango flavored breath.
I stood as a foreigner checked for passport
by the boundary wall of my house.
The gardener, the maid servant, my parents
all are potential banks for a smile loan.
The loan from the unknown girl
with the sunrise as a commercial adviser
proves public banks are still safer than private.

The Unrelenting Race

Yesterday's silhouettes
hanging from grips of postmodernism
race towards conclusion
through a ceaseless relay race

Exchanging arms-
each one tries to coagulate existence
radiating supremacy
from the showroom of breakups and make-ups.

It's a race with the crazy ox of devastation
twisting to verve from its effigy
chasing towards establishments with unified vision
and horns dipped in roots and soil.

With no master for the ox and no guide for the races
it's a challenge to
break walls, pierce crowds, deform irons
and
let the last drop of sweat drop fall on the ruins
of a wintry weather.

Performance For The Seventh Circle Of Hell

Against moss of ignominy
through a prancing multitude
in front of shuddering speakers
and livid roars, our concert
were like a smoked beehive.

The cement bridge of emotions
made flimsy by those demanding bites
made it sway in the cosmos of
blending cultures and sliding bodies.

Friction was a common muse
while I flew into Hell
circling past men fixed a trees
waiting for fools to cut them off
and build another stage to prance upon
and reserve a permit to the seventh circle.

(a ticket that doesn't demand cash
but just a few unruly performances
we smile at and later muse upon)

On The Rocks

Strolling ice cubes throw bubbles
into the vapor stricken world
while a frozen river waits
for the bubbles to break and fall as tears.

Howling wolves plagued by the cultivation of smoke
howls ...howls...
Alas! their voices fail
to penetrate those cubes and the river.

(The voices) just flow down the glass of lords
and lie as slaves in front of the gleaming wine.

Journey through uneven terrains sought for words that would speak not for themselves, but for a being, fatigued but roaming. That is why **Sujan Bhattacharyya** took up his pen to frame words in their own perspective. Intercepted with busy hours as a state service officer, he looks back and forth to get the horizon with his words. He wants to speak to the surrounding not in a delicate manner, but to cater words that want to mean something. His poems in English have already appeared in *Blue Cygnus* and *Solstice Poetry*. His poems have recently been published in the global anthologies on Nelson Mandela and World Peace, published by Inner Child Press, limited (U.S.A.). He has two titles of poetry in Bengali named, *Nishkranto Okshar* (*Emerged Words*) and *Shobder Valobasa* (*Love For Words*) and a collection of stories in Bengali *Gogon Dhakir Rokto* (*Blood of Gogon, The Drummer*).

Destiny

All these funeral sticks
Will call me in the flow of fumes dark.
As all the fore-fathers are in rest
In the tender youth of these spiral days,
All the molecules—
Who are known to be of mine—
Shall pass on to an address unknown.

The ruins left will nowhere embrace my name,
Neither any field of crops
Will hold the foot-print of mine—
Fatigued of the journeyed path.

The more as I move down the dusk
The more I shall be remaining
 In the wings of sparrows vibrant.

Get Changed

Dress up with newer days,
In the desire bewildered
Go on smashing the personal wall
And each the pieces it's of colorful bricks
That liked to give you signals
Of the delicate path
That leads to the hell, of one's own.

Step up here now
Come up to the fence
Get changed within your corpus and soul,
Go on changing
Day by day
And thus
Make the surroundings changed.

Are You

Can you be a fire, the sacrificial flame?
Can you put all the selected hours into the feast
Of your love omnivorous
In the commitment of tranquility
That slays the darkness to the last?

You never have wanted to become water;
Didn't want to draw yourself in the jubilant blue
Seeking kisses from mosses
In the cold affinity of a swirl.

You never wanted to become water
Nor a complacent sky.
You never tried to be a shadow,
Never dreamt of flying like a silent bird.

Can you be a fire –
An inferno
On the bank of a darkest night!

Myself

Never have I seen any unique dream,
Never have I uttered any secret phrase
Holding any galaxy in my palms.
Each of the nocturnal transcriptions
Has widened me in the shadow of shrubs.
Has adorned me
With the worn out reports of the autumn.

Never have I sought any assurance from a well-versed stream,
Never have embraced any forest virgin.
Never have looked for a shelter in the words nascent.

To the certain destiny
Incessant, I just simply flow,
In the unconcerned solitude let I remain myself
Ousted, at an unapproachable distance
From the surrounding that maddens.

Sutapa Chaudhuri is a bilingual poet writing in English and Bengali, an academic and a translator based in Kolkata, India, Dr. Sutapa Chaudhuri has studied at the Calcutta University, India and the Wayne State University, U.S.A. Currently she is Assistant Professor in English at Dr. Kanailal Bhattacharyya College, Howrah, and Guest Lecturer at the Dept. of English, University of Calcutta, West Bengal, India. Dr. Chaudhuri has several publications, critical and creative, in a number of reputed literary journals, magazines, webzines and books to her credit. *Broken Rhapsodies* (2011) is her first book of poems. She can be contacted at sutapachaudhuri8@gmail.com

Maheyi

101

Come, let us go home now mother,
Mother, my mother, Mother Earth—
Come, enfold me in your loving arms,
Let me sleep a little, secure and safe.
The harsh tyrannies of life—
Enough, they'll haunt me no more.
Come, mother, let us rest a while—
Nestled in your bosom, snug and warm
Let me dream a little
Elusive dreams of love and warmth.
Raging, scorching flames
Engulfed me twice,
Powerless yet to thaw
My ice, frozen solid, as you too.

We've suffered much, mother, you and I
Your stifled cries rent the terrible night
They dug the furrow deep into you
The deathly drone, the dark moment,
The dull throb of pain, the dripping redness
Flooding the dusk suddenly
The look of terror dilating
Your fathomless black eyes
The shrill shriek
Strangling your pristine virgin soil
Contorted, convulsed in inscrutable pain;
Yet, unheeding, they tore you apart
And snatched me up, ruthless—
A bloodied, quivering mass of flesh
Amidst a handful of dirt.

Maheyi, daughter of the earth—
Stripped off my name
Branded anew, *Janaki*,

Prized possession for a mighty patriarch.
Possessed, powerless, puppet-like—
They carried me away, a rag doll.
Swathed in their clothes,
Shorn of my truth, orphaned and cold,
Sita, the furrowed girl, unwanted, uprooted
Crying out dimly in mother-want
Separated, lonely in an unknown orbit;
Yet, just a spectacle, ever on display
Still another spoil of victory

You lay helpless, mother, abandoned, forgotten,
Crying silently in the shivering night
Frozen tears gnawing your parched red earth.
Mother, my mother, Mother Earth—
Bleeding, wounded, ripped apart.
Alien seeds forcefully planted
The torn, quivering womb, open, helpless
Invaded, emptied of its own
Nurtured so lovingly…
Enough! They'll hurt us no more
Their cruel hands
Powerless to reach us
We're safe now, mother, you and I,
We're home.

Red

red is the color of
life—
life,
pulsating,
surging through
youthful beauty—
a warm gush
staining aglow
the lips vibrant;
the cheeks
alive with color.
a soft radiant hue
lingering behind,
loitering,
nurturing warmth
in desire.

red is the color of
the mother's womb—
tiny petite butterflies
cocooned
in a sea of love.
the small bodies
nestle, curled up—
the eyes, the fists
yet unopened, unknowing
secure in an elemental trust;
a tenderness beaming—
nourishing love
forever…
yet, red is not for me;
in my arid world
lifeless
anemia reigns.

Colors Of Life

Colors are not my style.
life lived in black and white
bursts forth in wide spectrums
of myriad hues
forever free in connotative metaphors...

I too dwell in Possibility—

Who remains satisfied with a single color
catching on to you unawares—
defining, de-limiting possibilities,
coloring the shades of life
in a single staid solidarity.

The Light Of The Street Lamps

only the street lights on guard,
loneliness, like lost cubes of ice,
floats irrelevant, aimless
on the surface of forgotten life.
the deserted streets a silent witness to
a pair of spectacles, rimmed with black
left behind on a last journey.
discarded, lonely, like a half finished
bottle of rum, the left over cards on a skillet
loiter unloved with empty spaces.
forlorn in its corner, insignificant,
the unused toothbrush gathers dust.
out of place, the bared dentures
grow moldy in a senseless smile—
the once beloved scooter,
seats worn out with use
sifts through fond memories.
the silhouette of a night prowler
mar the still knife-edge of darkness—.
the diffused light of the street lamps
the only illumination in a play of
silent shadows.

Ananya S Guha is writer, poet and critic. He has six collections of poetry and several of his poems have appeared in anthologies such as The Harper Collins Book Of Poetry, Anthology of North East Poetry, Indo Australian Anthology Of Poetry etc. Among his book of poems are: What Else Is Alive (Writers Workshop Calcutta), A Hill Station And Other Poems (Minerva Press), Dusk Descends from Erbacce Press UK etc. His poems have been published in : The Telegraph , The Statesman, Amrita Bazar Patrika, Sunday Mail, Femina, Poeisis, Brown Critique, Poetry Chronicle, Poetry Chain, New Quest, Indian Literature, Chandrabhaga, Kavya Bharati, Kritya, Muse India, Other Voices, Poetry Soul To Soul, Lip Service, Poem Today, Asia Writes, Malaysian Poetic Chronicles, Up The Staircase, Decades Review, Poetry Five, eFiction India, The Amistad Journal Of English Literature, Glasgow Review, Shoe Horn Review Gloom Cupboard, Art Arena etc. He has translated contemporary Bengali poets into English, and some of the translations have been published in Journals such as Chandrabhaga. Other publications include: The Four Quarters Magazine, Lakeview etc.

He has written articles for journals, magazines and newspapers on social and educational matters. He also writes for children and many of his poems are up on BoloKids. He has been born and brought up in Shillong and has been working in the Indira Gandhi National Open University for the last twenty years. He holds a doctoral degree on the novels of William Golding.

Get This Away

Get this away
this away my highness
and the pond shrunk
still holds the lotus
in cupped hands
the river is life
whispers in eternity
about water, water, water
no not the ravage it causes, or deaths
or news in television channels

get this away, this away.

I Have Been Thinking Of Ghosts

I have been thinking of ghosts
ever since grandmother spoke
of the pond near our house
in Gauhati. Someone would walk across
it like a mesmeric shadow.

Then her two sons, choleric were seen flying
like sails on mast.

Now, I don't think of ghosts anymore.
Only grandmother who crossed her hundreds
and her paralytic fit.

Your Eyes

Your eyes
a love poem
your eyes
a haven for all dreams
your eyes, my evening song
your eyes, colors
into which I wade deep
and play the game of *Holi*!

City Of Love

In Calcutta
I only take my
wash bath
and hum soft tunes
to the city of love.

Bina Sarkar Ellias is founder-editor, designer and publisher of International Gallerie (www.gallerie.net), the award-winning global arts and ideas journal published from India since 1997. Engaged in socio-political and community building issues, she received a Fellowship in 2007 from the Asia Leadership Fellow Program and Japan Foundation for research and development of the project: Unity in Diversity. Envisioning Community Building in Asia and Beyond, 2007, the Times Group Yami Women Achiever's award in 2008, and the FICCI/FLO 2013 award for excellence in her work. Her poems have appeared in various magazines, anthologies and online poetry sites, besides, her chapbook of poems, *The Room* has been published by AarkArts, UK, and have been translated into German and Arabic. She has also read her poems at various venues. She has curated "Transitions 2010", a virtual event of visual, literary, and performing arts for The Pen and Brush, Inc", USA, a 119 years old organization, two group shows: 'Rain' at Sakshi Art Gallery, Mumbai, and 'Kashmir, besides a solo for artist Chinthala Jagdish at Tao Art Gallery, Mumbai, and a recent group show with 30 Indian artists, "Tagore Lost and Found", at Art Bull Gallery, New Delhi. Her forthcoming show with Kerala artists is scheduled for later this year.

A writer since the early seventies, she has contributed on socio-political issues and the arts to major national newspapers in the last forty years, *The Times of India, Indian Express* and *The Hindu*. She has been invited twice to chair discussions at the New Moves Festival in Glasgow, as well as speak at other forums in San Francisco, New York, Frankfurt, Tokyo, London, Tehran, Kabul, Karachi, Lahore, Santiniketan, Kolkata, Delhi and Mumbai. Bina Sarkar Ellias lives and works in Mumbai, India.

A River

a river
once ran

through
my girlhood

bearing boats
and fish

and laughing
broods

of naked
children

browned by
365 suns~

days of
innocence

unsullied
as its water.

today
the river

has met
the ocean,

its pure
white foam

bears

treasures

of lost
islands,

fruit of
the womb,

and shoals
of kinship.

the river
now is ocean,

the ocean
is sky,

the sky
my skin ~

a nimbus
of light.

Santiniketan 1

in Santiniketan
the red road rolls out, astonished ~
like Kali's tongue.

Santiniketan 2

and there it was~
choreographed on
a blue-black night,
a poet's storm
in delirium
as the trees swayed
and danced
with a wind gone mad~
and leaves swirled
in a dervish dance
and the first rain
washed the earth,
the red earth
of Santiniketan,
mourning the death
of its renaissance.

Dust

(Bangladesh, March 8, 2011)

dust in the wind
dust in the eyes
dust in the mind
dust in disguise.

dust by the river
dust by the sea
dust like a stalker
stalks eerily.

dust on the trees
dust-choked leaves
dust in the alleys
like daylight thieves.

dust in the whispers
dust in the screams
dust-faced swindlers
dust in their dreams.

a nation of dust
swallows the poor
a nation of lust
rots to the core

where ngo lords
rake in their loot
and ministers hoard
and judges are mute.

dust in the laughter
dust in the pain
dust is a tumor
in the nation's vein.

Rupendra Guha Majumdar is the Associate Professor, Department of English, Delhi University, India. He has been a Visiting Fulbright Fellow in the English Department at Yale University in 1981 and 1992. He has published four books of poetry in English-language from Writers Workshop, Calcutta: *Blunderbuss* (1971), *Apu's Initiation* (1975), *Tomcat* (1980), *The Hiroshima Clock* (1990). His poems have featured in several anthologies in India and abroad: *Modern English Poetry in India*, ed. P. Lal (1971); *Indo-English Poetry in Bengal*, ed. K.C. Lahiri (1974); *The Oxford Book of Animal Poems*, ed. Michael Harrison & Christopher Smart-Clark (London: Oxford UP, 1992); *Spotlight on Poetry: Poems around the World 3*, ed. Brian Moses & David Orme (London: Harper Collins, 1999); *The Golden Treasury of Writers Workshop Poetry* (2009), ed. Rubana Huq. Rupendra has translated Tagore's Bengali play, *Roktokorobi* (*Red Oleanders*) into English for *The Essential Tagore* (Vishwa Bharati Press & Harvard University Press, 2011); has contributed articles to *World Poetry From 1900 to the Present*, ed. R. Victor Arana, (New York, 2007). He lives in Delhi with his wife, Karabi, a social anthropologist, and their two sons, Mrittunjoy and Tirthankar.

Himalayan Chronicle And/Or Cityscape

1

Between your stories of life and death
you pause for me to catch up on the mossy
trail. I cannot measure the precarious mood
of pain you offer unto the day ,
I merely listen,
                catching my breath.

You say you have left behind you
the apple-orchards, the, rare blue hill-tops
        of Kinnaur in your mind, tucked
them under summer clouds with care

as you would tuck Dadi and Nana into bed,
touch their closed eyelids, their still smiling
lips in sleep with your deft, grass-cutting fingers.

Like the hill-tops, they are now far away
ensconced in clouds, clothed in rain and wind
and the swirling snow in a corner if the sky where
                no shadows stir.

Himalayan Chronicle And/Or Cityscape

2

In the city, with a brand new AC fitted into
the wall of your shared apartment just
below the window in the rear, you take on
the summer's heat head on (the landlord has
of course helped all along).
                           But what good is that
if you still need to sleep below the stars
and trees on the terrace to keep yourself cool;
and the curious sky descending from above
to whisper words of surprise into your ears,
ruffling your musk stained hair.

You say, looking askance, it helps you to sleep
 when you count one by one the clouds
                  leaping over meandering fences.
You return from the kitchen with a plate
of chopped watermelon, chunks of blazing
red sweetness that I can take in measures only,
if at all, as the doctor ordered; the rest is for
         you to have or to return
to the good earth as seedlings for tomorrow's sun,
                pulses of a summer's passion.

The south-west monsoon has gained
momentum deflecting heat from the flanks
          of the seventh city.
The clouds burst upon us
           carrying memories of snow
swirling around the crowns of distant hill-tops,
the smiles of slow, fulfilled aging
               merging into sleep.

Landscape With A Peepul Tree

In the scope of the teakwood frame
and even beyond, peepul leaves smudge
the sky with their print-block triangles
of lively green, each with two corners
rounded off deftly and one left to narrow
            down with a wiggle of a tail
till the tip releases upon
        your unwary eye (as you look up with
head thrown back) a drop of darkened
rain.

 Lips open for more respite after
days of primal thirst; a grim fumbling with
rosaries of Tulsi beads and marathon
prayers to the ultimate Investigator of Dreams,
haloed up high, bearing myriad names
that along with endnotes for the chosen tale
would fill up an Appendix portion
in the concluding pages of your definitive text.

The leaves are His words of intent(we are
told) inscribed in Nature, pronounced in
 whispers and in the running brooks;
        and the thin stalk of each leaf woven into
the trajectory of branches with the wind's
full monsoon concurrence riding by.

As paintbrushes newly awake, feature in
their own ways for once, endorse shades
of death, the branches untether mountains
of clouds, blue clouds of mountains, shrill,
homeward-calling birds, shepherd, flocks,
colors cascading from the shoulders
of the earth-descending sun into the distraught

        valley of lost flowers;

              all within the inclement sweep of
a Ramkinkar-landscape in Santhal oils
and local ingredients on a stretched canvas, six
by four, mounted and framed in bamboo, displayed
in a gallery meant for passersby and those
ebony princesses with no kingdoms or
to call their own, just the sky brimming over
 with the turbulence of peepul leaves
 and branches
                      swaying above an illegible signature
of sorts which   crouches in one corner,
            listening
                      to the wind.

Siddhartha Bose is a poet, playwright and performer based in London. His poetry books are *Kalagora* (Penned in the Margins, 2010) and *Digital Monsoon* (Penned in the Margins, 2013). Siddhartha has been featured on BBC 4, BBC Radio 3 and was dubbed one of the 'ten rising stars of British poetry' by *The Times*. Siddhartha wrote, performed and toured a one-man play, also called *Kalagora*, which had an acclaimed run at Edinburgh Festival Fringe 2011. His theatre show, *London's Perverted Children*, was long-listed for an Oxford Samuel Becket Theatre Trust award, and his new play, *The Shroud*, tours in 2014. He is currently completing an ethnographic film on Mumbai, and his PhD on the grotesque is forthcoming later this year. Siddhartha has been a Leverhulme Fellow at the University of London and a recipient of awards from the Arts Council England.

Nocturne

You pet your cat with
rain, pumice, snakebite.

Chew cigarettes with the
cleverness of an acrobat.

Swallow locusts of snow in the
shallow of your hand.

The smell of a dream as you
brushed past me—

    (rituals—

        red robes, arched rock,
          stinking sun, broken sea

            a monk
            whipping the oil of fear in our
              moves)

—shifts the
      orbit of my needs.

One day-night, grace my hut
      twined in bees—
so a fool as me
      masked in tongues—
words of a prince on my lap—

could serve you a brim of tea,
      dance like a disease in your blood,
          smell ribbons of fire in your hair.

Lyrics

I

I dream you with a stranger—

Nails sharp, shrapneled, in the
Lamplight of a smoked, kleenexed room.

II

When he takes you
without shame—

grasshoppers glaring
through your window—

think my heart a stone,
skipping on your desire-pond,

a garden-weed.

III

In the end, what remains,
maims—

incense of your eyes,
fumes of your smile.

Elegy

The crack in your skull
reveals:

a love for a man
you hid in a
glass of gin.

A dog
doubting your good intentions.

Two stale photographs
of your sister's children.

Smackstains dotting your hands like
flies on meat in
Canal street.

Nipples packed with boils.

(New York City too is
packed with boils)

A belly too big to hold back the
oil and grease.

O Virgin Queen of Avenue C!

Now that it's late enough,
this is what they may

say of you.

Still Life

By reddish curtain—
                    bent in a chair—

                        breasts like dogs—

        nipples of tongues—
                            wagging towards a

            drum of cars

Nabina Das has authored a short fiction collection recently, *The House of Twining Roses: Stories of the Mapped and the Unmapped* (LiFi Publications, Delhi) and a poetry collection *Into the Migrant City* (Writers Workshop, Kolkata). Her debut novel *Footprints in the Bajra* (Cedar Books, Delhi) was long-listed in the prestigious "Vodafone Crossword Book Award 2011." An MFA from Rutgers University, U.S.A., and an MA from Jawaharlal Nehru University, Delhi, Nabina's debut poetry collection *Blue Vessel* (Les Editions du Zaporogue, Denmark) was nominated as one of the best of 2012. Her poetry and prose appear in several international journals and anthologies, the latest being *The Yellow Nib: Modern English Poetry by Indians*, Queen's University, Belfast. A contributor to the University of Nebraska-Lincoln's *Prairie Schooner* literary journal blog, Nabina is the winner of the *2012 Charles Wallace Fellowship in Creative Writing*, University of Stirling, UK, and the *2012 Sangam House Lavanya Sankaran Fiction Fellowship* besides other prizes in major national poetry contests. With a background in journalism and media, Nabina is trained in Indian classical music. She teaches Creative Writing in classrooms and workshops, and occasionally blogs at nabinadas13.wordpress.com

The Meeting

Because it's noon
Because it's hot
With high sun
Because he's here
Because I stare
We say hello
His hands terracotta
His forehead balsam
His mouth lemony
Sing La Marseillaise
He whispers slow
Sing with me
Painted letters red
His hand holds
This bold placard
Swift and sad
The cafeteria hums
The sun thumps
On still windowsills
We feel together
The rebels inside
Let them speak
Song to song
Hand to hand
Words of meeting
Words of passion
Watch how then
We melt inside
With phrases pure
The magic minutes.

All I Want Is You

On the sepia pages a never-ending story
On my cherry desk an ink inscribing only deep love
On the swept porch a wind-chime speaking your voice
On my head, a swear word, a mouthful, I'd never want to forget
In the placid shower a purer Ganga streaming
In my photoshopped dreams a bright collage unpainted
In the night sky a foreign moon crafted of unknown softness
In the mornings a ray bright enough lighting up all three worlds
By my running gear the throb of your heart
By my coffee cup an addiction stranger and darker
By the roadside a pretty pebble for my diamond-less ring
By my side your face, a legend that says Shakespeare's never been
in love
All I want is you.

Viewing Kanchenjunga

He and I, uneven, would go up the winding path
Streaming from the front of that sleepy house
He tall, me very short and running to catch up
With long strides of my uncle's morning walk.
"It's the third highest mountain peak you'll see
In a while," he lectured, and I half heard, busy,
Too busy tweaking dew drops off crisp arum leaves
And a taut red hibiscus straining to see the sun.
He would climb the little hillock easily, quick,
I scampering off like a poodle on a tight leash.
More scholarship booming at the blinky sky would
Have clouds yawning faraway. "Know what are the
Gold, silver, gems, grain and holy books? Ah-ha,
Treasures! Five Treasures of Snows!" I would
Count birds waking, then fleeing the din at dawn
And the wave of his walking stick, jaunty laugh
To see the peak wake up and then he would leave.
I stayed a bit longer on the shiny hillock's crest
Before tumbling down. The treasured peak had to
Rise as high as my teeny scrawny dark head with
The sun, so I would finally see that thigh of gold bark.

Kiriti Sengupta is a professionally qualified Dental Surgeon from Calcutta, a bilingual poet, a widely published author (both in India and U.S.A.), and translator both in Bengali and English. He is the author of the bestselling title, *My Glass Of Wine*, a novelette based on autobiographic poetry. Kiriti's others works include: *My Dazzling Bards* (literary critiquing), *The Reciting Pens* (his interviews of three published Bengali poets along with his translations of a few of their poems), *The Unheard I* (widely reviewed literary nonfiction), *Desirous Water* (contributed as the translator), *Byakul Shabdo Kichu* (Bengali poetry), and *Aay Na* (Bengali nonfiction based on free verses). His poetry has appeared in several e-zines, *Tajmahal Review*, *The Hans India*, *Kritya*, and in international anthologies – *Heavens Above: Poetry Below* (Canada), and *Twist of Fate* (U.S.A.). His short stories (creative) have been published in *Labyrinth*, and an article on *Research Scholar*. Kiriti has been the 'joint editor' of the poetry anthology, *Scaling Heights*, published by Authors Press, New Delhi.

Details of his account can be accessed at: www.kiritisengupta.com

Water

An experiment I undertook. A seed slept in dark, clueless; no viable chant ... what if awakened by mantra? A syllable to prefix and suffix, and thus was my pride and prejudice! Got confined, even as I desire to move on. Now the pride is dear; dearer than my dearest...
#
Following some cunning way I was keen to taste some greatness. A tree stands with its green veil. Through its branches I noticed the ascent of sap, but it had no salt. Some names sweet ... some seeds added at source!
#
As one finds it apt! Just the way the mind seeks. My mind. Mantra bears lust ... petty you, you blame the luster! Lust reinstated ... inevitable it is...
#
Immersion via the mirror ... good bye to the goddess, but the lion keeps awake with his eyes closed. His eyes are terrific ... mesmerizing, or giving all as I surrender. The first involves mixing while the latter denotes craving!
#
Deviations bring popularity ... endless celebrations. Fists full of water and free donation ... serving the pilgrims. Withdrawal reversed...
#
Complete bath and a full dip ... no excuses, please ... be it the pollution sick! You sprinkle drops, however ... your wisdom runs into the lustrous hole. Incenses are not burn by wet hands, they say. Prohibited it is. Water has no call, no décor either; it floats the bone and frame free!

Celluloid

Gold is precious and so is the time
we spent together; right from the morning tea
spanning over the lavish lunch until you said,
"Signing off for today."
I was hesitant, you know, I never said goodbye.

Signs are private, and I keep my eyes
open round the clock!

Fish-Lip

I have read
morphology of the fish-lip
gives hint of the water color deep.

A small aquarium inside my living … cornered—
marks of love and kisses
on either side;
even on its face!

My lips are thin,
no trace of color, but
water….

Memorandum Of Understanding

I'm no linguist!

I know
air and age are linked
since eternity…

And the wounds surface again,
in all directions…
sporting the guise of youth…

Postscript

The Poetry Society of India has been founded by *Yayati* Madan G Gandhi some fifteen years back in Gurgaon, Haryana. A visiting fellow of St. John's College, Cambridge *Yayati* Madan G. Gandhi is an outstanding educationist, litterateur, philanthropist and publicist, who has been in the vanguard of many movements for sustainable environment, total disarmament, human rights and one-world mankind. A moving, powerful voice in contemporary English Poetry having a unique place in the world of mysticism and poetry for peace and a winner of 'Tagore Award' in poetry in 1961, Dr. Gandhi is the President of The Poetry Society of India. He is the author of twenty poetry titles that include *Ashes and Embers*, *Kundalini*, *Luteous Serpent*, *Petals of Flame*, *Freak Stair*, *Meandering Maze*, *Ring of Silence*, *Shunayata in Trance*, *Haiku and Quatrains*, *Enchanting Flute*, *The Imperilled Earth*, *Planet in Peril: Poet's Lament*, *Parvrajya Peals*. His magnum opus *The Imperilled Earth* has been reviewed by many leading intellectuals of the world. Khushwant Singh, the late journalist and litterateur has had profusely quoted from the book in his column "This Above All," published in *Indian Express* and many other national dailies on January 1, 1994. Singh had complimented the poet for making a forceful plea against the impending dangers of nuclear holocaust and environmental degradation and his wanting man to withdraw from the precipice well in time. Gandhi's latest work has been the poetic rendering of Guru Nanak Dev's *Japuji Sahib* published by Gandhi Earth Vision Foundation in 2010. In a befitting recognition of his excellence in poetry, World Academy of Arts and Culture conferred, in 1993, the honorary degree of Doctor of Litterateur (Litt. D) upon Gandhi for making a distinguished contribution for promoting world order and international understanding through his writings. Georges Friedenkraft has listed him among the prominent poets of India, and has translated his *Dance of Life* into French.

Mission Statement

• To promote the spirit of poetry and to foster poetic talent among people all ages.

• To give encouragement to young budding poets and honor those who have distinguished themselves as creative writers.

• To set up a poets' cooperative for the publication of their works and exploring avenues for globalised distribution.

• To arrange poetry workshops, poetic symposiums, seminars and conferences on the art and craft of poetry and to solve the contemporary crises through the medium of poetry.

• To launch a benevolent fund to render help to indigent and needy poets and to succor the families of poets struck with sudden calamity.

• To arrange to bring out on no profit no loss basis a series of poetry anthologies of member poets and to launch a bimonthly journal on poetry, if the members so decide.

• To establish and maintain contacts with other institutions and organizations, governmental and non-governmental, cultural and literary work, and to enlist their cooperation in the furtherance of the objects of the society.

• To raise funds for the execution and the furtherance of these objects.

Members

Founder-President, and Editor-In Chief: Madan Gandhi (*Yayati*)
Secretary: Kiriti Sengupta
Assistant Secretary: Prabir Roy
Managing Editor-cum-Director: Sushma Devayani Dervish
Website Manager: Rishab Trivedi
Publication Manager: Shashi Kant Sharma
Editorial Board: Bibu Padhi, Vinod Khanna, Jaydeep Sharangi, Gopakumar Radhakrishnan, Indira Babbellapati, Sarala Ram Kamal, Ramakanta Das, Tapeshwar Prasad, Preeth Nambiar, Kanchan Bhattacharya, Nandini Sahu, Jernail S Anand

9 789383 888115